Sport and Entertainment

Sport and Entertainment

Brian Williams

Miles Kelly
PUBLISHING

Author
Brian Williams

Designed, Edited and Project Managed by
Starry Dog Books

Editor
Belinda Gallagher

Assistant Editor
Mark Darling

Artwork Commissioning
Lesley Cartlidge

Indexer
Janet De Saulles

Art Director
Clare Sleven

Editorial Director
Paula Borton

First published in 2001 by
Miles Kelly Publishing Ltd
The Bardfield Centre
Great Bardfield
Essex CM7 4SL

24681097531

Some material in this book can also be found in *The Greatest Book of the Biggest and Best*

A British Library Cataloguing-in-Publication Data.
A catalogue record for this book is available from the British Library

ISBN 1-84236-063-9

Printed in China

www.mileskelly.net
info@mileskelly.net

CONTENTS

SPORT AND

ENTERTAINMENT

For thousands of years, people have taken part in sports. The very first Olympic Games took place in Greece 776 BC, and still take place today. The 21st century still enjoys the thrill of sport, but people also find entertainment in thousands of other pastimes.

From roller coaster riding to rock climbing, to snowboarding and playing giant chess, people love to do different things. For instance, collecting things like teddy bears can be pretty popular – and expensive – someone once paid £110,000 for one – rather a lot of money for a cuddly toy!

Explore the biggest and best facts of *Sport and Entertainment* and enjoy your very own roller coaster ride. There are serious facts – for reference – and less serious ones, too, for fun. These pages are packed with the biggest and best, oddest and strangest, smallest and funniest facts around!

◀ ATHLETIC TRACK EVENT

PLAYING GAMES

For more than 5,000 years people have played games. Some of the earliest were board games and games of chance, using dice or pieces like dominoes. The ancient Egyptians enjoyed wrestling and chariot racing, and Greek athletes took part in the Olympic Games more than 3,000 years ago. The rules of many modern games, such as tennis and rugby football, were drawn up in the 1800s. Today some stars are paid more than the leaders of their countries!

▲ Polo – the name comes from the Persian word 'pulu' – was first played 5,000 years ago in India, and then Persia. Hitting a ball from a horse's back gave cavalry soldiers expert training at controlling their horses.

» OLDEST GAMES AND SPORTS		
	GAME OR SPORT	FIRST PLAYED
1	Wrestling	3000 BC
2 =	Horse racing	2500 BC
2 =	Dice	2500 BC

◀ Sumo wrestling is popular in Japan. Size is important – the heaviest wrestlers weigh more than 200 kg. The heaviest-ever sumo champion, from Hawaii, weighed a body-crushing 267 kg!

» MOST FAMOUS ALL-TIME GREATS		
Basketball	Michael Jordan	USA
Cricket	Sir Donald Bradman	Australia
Soccer	Pelé	Brazil
Golf	Jack Nicklaus	USA
Boxing	Muhammad Ali*	USA

Note: *Muhammad Ali was voted most famous sports star of the 20th century

▲ Eldrick 'Tiger' Woods of the USA won the world's four major golf titles (the British and US Opens, the US Masters and the US PGA) by the age of just 24. He was only the fifth person to achieve this 'Grand Slam', and he was also the youngest.

RICHEST SPORTS STARS (ESTIMATED YEARLY EARNINGS)			
	NAME	SPORT	EARNINGS
1	Michael Jordan	Basketball	£40 million +
2 =	Michael Schumacher	Racing driver	£30 million
2 =	'Tiger' Woods	Golfer	£30 million

▲ American football has been played by professional teams in the National Football League since 1922. Championship of the league is decided in the annual Super Bowl game, a major sports spectacle since 1967, watched by millions of viewers worldwide.

GAME, SET AND MATCH

● Using a modern tennis racket with a fibreglass-graphite frame and tightly strung synthetic strings, a top male player can serve the ball at over 220 km/h.

TOUGHEST CHALLENGE

● The Ironman Triathlon was first held in Hawaii in 1978. Contestants have to swim 4 km, ride a bike for 180 km and then run a marathon.
● After 8 hours only the very fittest triathletes are still running!

▲ Chess, shown here being played with giant pieces, was played at least 1,500 years ago. It probably began in India. The first world champion was William Steinitz of Austria, who held the title from 1866 to 1894.

IT'S A FACT
Some games have not changed in hundreds of years. In Children's Games, painted in 1560 by Pieter Bruegel, children are shown playing with hoops and riding piggyback.

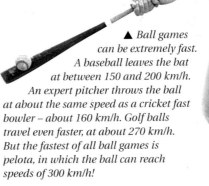

▲ Ball games can be extremely fast. A baseball leaves the bat at between 150 and 200 km/h. An expert pitcher throws the ball at about the same speed as a cricket fast bowler – about 160 km/h. Golf balls travel even faster, at about 270 km/h. But the fastest of all ball games is pelota, in which the ball can reach speeds of 300 km/h!

SOCCER GREATS

Soccer is the world's biggest spectator sport. The only continent where it does not reign supreme is North America. Both China and Europe claim to have invented football, which developed into soccer, now watched by millions of people around the world. Europe's top clubs, such as Manchester United (England), Real Madrid (Spain) and Internazionale-Milan (Italy), are so rich that they can afford to pay over £30 million for just one star player. The biggest international soccer tournament is the World Cup, held every four years.

◄ *Many children dream of playing soccer for their country, and for the fame and money that stardom can bring. In richer countries children are taught from a young age. In poorer countries they play wherever there is a patch of ground and a ball.*

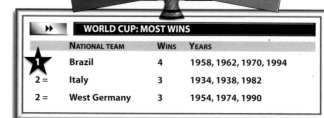

►► WORLD CUP: MOST WINS		
NATIONAL TEAM	**WINS**	**YEARS**
Brazil	4	1958, 1962, 1970, 1994
Italy	3	1934, 1938, 1982
West Germany	3	1954, 1974, 1990

◄ *Brazil's soccer star Pelé, real name Edson Arantes do Nascimento, is rated the greatest player of all time. Born in 1940, Pelé played in three World Cup-winning sides, in 1958, 1962 and 1970. Pelé scored his 1,000th goal during his 909th first-class match, and his total when he retired in 1977 was a remarkable 1,281 goals in 1,363 games!*

THE TOPS

● The first World Cup, held in Uruguay in 1930, was won by Uruguay.

● Brazil has the biggest football stadium in the world. The Maracana Municipal Stadium in Rio de Janeiro can hold 205,000 fans.

● Brazil are the only team to have won the World Cup four times.

▼ *Old Trafford in Manchester is the home of Manchester United, the world's richest club. In 1999 United won the English Premier League, the FA Cup and the European Champions Cup.*

»	**£30+ MILLION PLAYERS**		
	NAME	**TRANSFER**	**FEE**
1	**Luis Figo**	**Barcelona to Real Madrid**	**£37.4 million**
2	**Hernan Crespo**	**Parma to Lazio**	**£36 million**
3	**Christian Vieri**	**Lazio to Inter-Milan**	**£31 million**

Note: all these deals were done in 2000

3-tier seating

pitch

▼ *The World Cup trophy is presented to the winning team every four years. Countries qualify for the final stages through an elimination series. Brazil are the only nation to have played in every World Cup finals stage.*

seating for 67,000 spectators

entrance

luxury boxes

◄ *The 1994 World Cup tournament was the first to be staged in the United States. The winners were Brazil, shown here in yellow and blue playing against Italy in blue and white. Brazil took the trophy for the fourth time.*

OLYMPIC GAMES

The Olympic Games is the biggest international sports competition on Earth. Thousands of athletes, representing nearly every country in the world, come together every four years to take part in individual and team sports. A few take home gold, silver or bronze medals. New sports are added at every Games, and billions of people watch the Olympics on television. Separate Winter Games for winter sports such as skiing and ice skating are also held every four years at snowy locations.

▲ *The first recorded Olympic Games were held at Olympia in Greece in 776 BC. They were held every four years after that until AD 393. Athletes entered the 20,000-capacity stadium through this stone arch.*

◀ *Relays of runners carry a flaming torch from Greece to the country where the Olympic Games are to be held. In the opening ceremony the torch is used to light the Olympic flame, a beacon that burns until the Games are over.*

▶▶ SUPER-OLYMPIANS			
Carl Lewis	USA	9 golds in track and field	1984–96
Jesse Owens	USA	4 golds in track and field	1936
Mark Spitz	USA	7 golds in swimming	1972
Vera Caslavska	CZK	7 golds in gymnastics	1964–68
Steve Redgrave	GBR	5 golds in rowing	1984–2000
Raymond Ewry	USA	10 golds in track and field*	1900–08

Note: * = the most by any competitor

DID YOU KNOW?
In ancient Greece athletes often competed naked. (Women were not allowed to watch or take part!) Greek artists strove to capture the athletes' grace and power in works of sculpture. This famous statue is a Roman copy of a Greek statue called The Discus-thrower, *made about 450 BC. The ancient Greeks used a bronze plate for their discus.*

◀ *Long jumper Bob Beamon (USA) set an amazing world record in 1968 at the Mexico City Olympics by leaping 8.9 m. This added 78 cm to the Olympic record. His world record lasted until 1991.*

➤➤	TOP FIVE GOLD WINNERS	
	COUNTRY	GOLDS
★1	USA	931
2	Russia*	572
3	Germany**	470
4	France	207
5	GBR	195

Note: Summer Games since 1896, Winter Games since 1924. * = USSR until 1992; ** = East and West Germany from 1968 to 1988

▶ *After 1,500 years the Olympic Games were revived. The 1896 Games were held in the Greek capital, Athens, in the stadium shown here. The Games have been held every four years since 1896, except during wartime (1916, 1940 and 1944).*

▶ *An Olympic gold medal is the most sought-after award in sport. The winner's national anthem is played as the medal is presented, and silver and bronze medals are given to the athletes who come second and third.*

▼ *In the 110-m and 400-m hurdles races, athletes such as Colin Jackson must exercise perfect balance, concentration and fitness. They also need flexible hip joints and strong thigh muscles to protect their knees on impact.*

➤➤	TOP AT SYDNEY 2000		
	COUNTRY	GOLDS	MEDALS
★1	USA	39	97
2	Russia	32	88
3	China	28	59
4	Australia	16	58
5	Germany	14	57
6	France	13	38
7	Italy	13	34
8	Netherlands	12	25
9	Cuba	11	29
10	GBR	11	28
11	Romania	11	26
12	South Korea	8	28
13	Hungary	8	17
14	Poland	6	14
15	Japan	5	18
16	Bulgaria	5	13
17	Greece	4	13
18	Sweden	4	12
19	Norway	4	10
20	Ethiopia	4	8
21	Ukraine	3	23
22	Belarus	3	17
23	Canada	3	14
24	Spain	3	11
25	Kazakhstan	3	7

Atlanta 1996

HOBBIES AND PASTIMES

A hobby is something people do for fun and not because they have to. In prehistoric times people were too busy finding food and shelter to have hobbies. It was only when survival became easier and people had time to spare that hobbies and pastimes developed. Early pastimes included drawing, sewing, riding and dancing. Today people fill their leisure time with fishing, cycling, collecting (anything from Beanies to Pokémon cards), making models, playing computer games and Internet surfing.

◀ Birdwatchers, or 'twitchers', go to extraordinary lengths to spot a bird they have not seen before. Some twitchers have spotted more than 8,000 of the 9,000 or so species.

▼ Fishing is one of the most popular pastimes worldwide. A monster catch like this record-breaking 700-kg marlin would need an extra-large case.

RECORD COLLECTIONS		
	COLLECTION	NUMBER
★1	Buttons	1 million
2	Bottle caps	82,000
3	Matchbox labels	74,000
4	Fridge magnets	15,000
5	Ties	10,000

▼ Windsurfing, or sailboarding, is a water sport that first became popular as a hobby in 1969. The sailboard is a surfboard with a sail. A sailboarder needs a good wind to send the board racing across the water.

◀ *The first jigsaw was cut out by mapmaker John Spilsbury in 1791. He wanted to make geography fun for children. The biggest-ever jigsaw had 44,000 pieces. Put together in France in 1992, it covered more than half a soccer pitch.*

IT'S A FACT
A penny stamp can be worth a million to a collector – if it is rare. A letter dated 1847 with two Mauritius stamps (original value 1 and 2 pence) sold in 1993 for over £2 million!

▶ *Model planes were flown in the 1800s, before full-sized ones. This giant model of a Russian* Antonov 225 *cargo plane, built in 1995, had a wing-span of over 5.6 m, but weighed only about 20 kg.*

foot-hold in rock

safety harness

▼ *Robot modelling is a popular hobby, especially in Japan. The latest robots, like this Lego Mindstorms character, use electronics and computers to react to the world around them.*

▶ *People have climbed mountains since ancient times, but modern climbing began in the 19th century. A skilled rock climber with modern equipment can scale sheer rock walls on which there seem to be no obvious hand- or foot-holds.*

COLLECTING BEARS

● Collecting can be an expensive hobby. In 1994 a Steiff bear was bought by a collector for £110,000, making it the most expensive teddy ever!

● Teddy bears were named after US President Theodore 'Teddy' Roosevelt.

SPEEDY SPORTS

Record speeds in sports are always being broken. Runners run ever faster, golf balls are hit farther and tennis players serve faster – thanks to a combination of training and technology. Before 1800, the speediest sports were horse racing, real tennis, fencing and archery. But following the inventions of the car and the aeroplane, a new craze was born – breaking speed records, whether in the air, on water or on land. The fastest team game at present is ice hockey, in which players zoom around the rink at up to 50 km/h, whacking the puck at 160 km/h.

▲ *A speed skater going flat out can whizz across the ice at about 60 km/h. But a sled or toboggan hurtling down an icy track is over twice as fast, reaching about 140 km/h. This is a bit faster than the fastest skateboard, which can reach 126 km/h with the rider lying on the board.*

SKYDIVING

● A skydiver falls through the air at 1,000 km/h before opening a parachute.
● In 1956 an American skydiver fell for an incredible 40 minutes, gliding on warm air currents.

▼ *The fastest racehorses gallop at a top speed of 69 km/h over a short 400-m flat sprint, just fast enough to outpace a racing greyhound. Speeds drop over longer races. Fast horses win big prizes – the Dubai World Cup race has a first prize of over £2 million.*

▲ *Ice hockey is a fast and furious game, with the heavily padded players crashing into one another on the ice while in pursuit of the puck – a rubber disc. Ice hockey was first played in Canada in the 1850s.*

▶ *Snowboarding is even faster than skateboarding. This 'extreme', or fast and sometimes dangerous, sport became a craze in the 1990s with people who wanted the thrill of skiing, but on a board. Other extreme sports, also called X-Games, include motocross and snow mountain bike riding.*

▼ *With a rocketlike serve of more than 200 km/h, US tennis star Pete Sampras won a record seventh Wimbledon singles title in 2000, his fourth win in a row. This broke the all-time record of 12 'grand-slam' title wins held by Australia's Roy Emerson (1961–67).*

➤➤	SPEEDY SPORTS COMPARED		
	PERSON OR OBJECT		**SPEED**
★ 1	Sky diver		1,000 km/h
2 =	Pelota ball		300 km/h
2 =	Racing motorbike		300 km/h
3	Golf ball		270 km/h
4	Tennis ball		220 km/h
5	Skier		210 km/h
6	Cricket ball (bowled)		160 km/h
7	Toboggan		140 km/h
8	Greyhound		67 km/h
9	Speed skater		60 km/h
10	Sprinter		37 km/h

◀ *Sailing is one of the oldest sports. The fastest sailing boats today are trimarans, which have three hulls, and catamarans, which have two. The record speed reached by a sailing vessel was 86 km/h on a 500-m run. But sailing on ice is even quicker. An ice yacht has been timed at speeds of more than 225 km/h!*

A GOOD READ

The oldest printed book dates from the AD 800s, but it was not until 1454, when Johannes Gutenberg set up Europe's first printing press, that books became available cheaply and in large numbers. The first book Gutenberg printed was the Bible, still the world's number-one bestseller. In 1935 the publisher Penguin started the paperback revolution. Today's most popular titles may be printed in millions, like the most-read children's books of the 1990s and 2000, the Harry Potter series by J. K. Rowling.

▲ *The Rosetta stone was found in Egypt in 1799. On it was the same inscription in three kinds of writing – ancient Egyptian picture-writing called hieroglyphic, demotic (a simpler form of Egyptian writing) and Greek. It gave scholars the key to understanding Egyptian hieroglyphs.*

◄ *The most famous detective in literature is Sherlock Holmes. Frequently mistaken by readers for a real person, Holmes and his friend Dr. Watson first appeared in Arthur Conan Doyle's story* A Study In Scarlet *in 1887.*

»	MOST QUOTED AUTHORS	
	NAME	**DATES**
1	William Shakespeare	1564–1616
2	Charles Dickens	1812–70
3	Sir Walter Scott	1771–1832
4	Johann Wolfgang von Goethe	1749–1832
5	Aristotle	384–322 BC

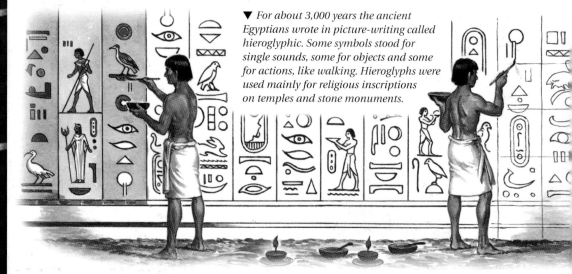

▼ *For about 3,000 years the ancient Egyptians wrote in picture-writing called hieroglyphic. Some symbols stood for single sounds, some for objects and some for actions, like walking. Hieroglyphs were used mainly for religious inscriptions on temples and stone monuments.*

◀ Braille is a raised-dot alphabet used by blind people. It is read by running the fingertips over the dots, or bumps. Braille was invented by a blind French teenager named Louis Braille in the 1820s.

▲ Charles Dickens (1812–70) was one of the most popular novelists of all time. His books such as A Christmas Carol and Oliver Twist are full of memorable characters, humour and sadness. Dickens gave public readings from his many books.

BESTSELLING BOOKS
BESTSELLERS
1 ★ The Bible
2 The plays of William Shakespeare
3 The Little Red Book of Mao Zedong

THE LONGEST WORD

● This is a ridiculously long chemical enzyme name that starts with *methionyl-* and ends in *-serine*. In between there are 1,894 other letters, making a total of 1,909!

▲ The first book printed using movable metal blocks of type was Johannes Gutenberg's Bible of 1456. The first printer in Britain was William Caxton, in 1476.

▶ Bede, an English monk who lived from about 673 to 735, is often called 'the Father of English History'. His written history of the English (731) is the best account of events in the years after the Romans left Britain.

DID YOU KNOW?
The Bible, parts of which were written more than 3,000 years ago, contains over 3.5 million words and is the world's biggest-selling book. The shortest verse in the Bible is John 11, verse 35: "Jesus wept".

▲ The biggest-selling writer ever is Agatha Christie (1890–1976). Her 78 crime stories, featuring detectives Hercule Poirot and Miss Marple, have been translated into more than 44 languages. Many have been made into plays such as The Mousetrap.

COMIC BOOK HEROES	
Dick Tracy	1931
Batman	1937
Desperate Dan, *Dandy*	1937
Superman	1938
Charlie Brown, *Peanuts*	1950
Dan Dare	1950

SOUNDS IMPRESSIVE

Music was first written down about 1800 BC. The three biggest groups of musical instruments are wind instruments, which are blown into, stringed instruments, which are plucked or played with a bow, and percussion instruments such as drums and cymbals, which are hit. They are used to play all kinds of music ranging from classical, opera and military to folk, jazz, pop and rock. Some of the most famous composers of 'classical' music wrote long pieces, called symphonies, for orchestras.

▶ *Drums are among the oldest of all musical instruments. The biggest drum kit ever built, in 1994, had over 300 pieces. Most drummers manage with less!*

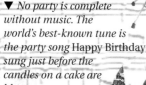

▼ *No party is complete without music. The world's best-known tune is the party song* Happy Birthday, *sung just before the candles on a cake are blown out.*

THREE GREAT COMPOSERS

Note: experts will never agree on 'the greatest-ever composer', but many music-lovers place the following as the top three:

Johann Sebastian Bach
(1865–1750)

Wolfgang Amadeus Mozart
(1756–91)

Ludwig van Beethoven
(1770–1827)

SPOOKY TUNES

● In 1964 Rosemary Brown 'composed' music she said was played for her by Frans Liszt, a Hungarian pianist who died in 1886. His ghost, she said, moved her hands over the piano. She also produced music in the style of Beethoven, Chopin and Schubert.

▶ *The violin was developed from earlier stringed instruments. The finest violins were made in Italy by Antonio Stradivari in the 1600s.*

▶ *The saxophone was the invention of Adolphe Sax of Belgium. He made the first one about 1840.*

▼ *The violoncello, usually called a cello, is really a big violin. It dates from the 1600s, about the same time as the violin.*

◀ *The guitar's origins go back to ancient Egypt, but the shape of the Spanish acoustic guitar, shown here, dates from the 1800s. Most guitars have 6 strings, but some have 12. Guitars used by ex-rock stars sell for huge sums of money.*

◀ *Instruments do not get much longer than the alpenhorn. This 4-m-long wooden horn was used by herdsmen in the Swiss Alps to communicate across mountain valleys.*

▼ *In a standard concert orchestra as many as 100 musicians play more than 20 different kinds of instrument. But in 1998, in Birmingham, UK, 3,503 musicians played a piece by composer Malcolm Arnold!*

➤➤ LONGEST AND QUIETEST MUSICAL EXPERIENCES			
Longest opera	*Die Meistersinger...*	R. Wagner	5 hrs, 15 mins
Longest symphony	*Symphony No.2*	H. Brian	1 hr, 39 mins
Quietest piece	4'33"	J. Cage	4 mins silence
Longest applause	For singer Placido Domingo		1 hr, 20 mins

ROCKING RECORDS

The first rock superstar was Elvis Presley, 'The King' of rock 'n' roll. Such is his popularity that although he died in 1977, there are still more than 600 fan clubs and countless lip-curling lookalikes! In the 1960s the Beatles took the world by storm and became the biggest-selling group of all time. More recent superstars include Mariah Carey, the first singer to hit the Top 5 with her first ten singles. Carey, Madonna and Whitney Houston are the biggest-selling female singers, each with over 45 platinum (million-selling) albums.

▲ *Mississippi-born singer Elvis Presley (1935–77) became the first pop superstar. Nicknamed 'Elvis the Pelvis' for his hip-twitching on stage, he made rock 'n' roll popular all over the world.*

▼ *In the 1960s 'Beatle-mania' swept the world. The Beatles, from left to right: Paul McCartney, Ringo Starr, George Harrison and John Lennon, sold more recordings than any other performers, topped the US charts 20 times, and made number 1 in the UK 17 times – a record they share with Elvis Presley.*

»	HUGE HITS OF THE 20TH CENTURY		
White Christmas	1942	Bing Crosby	Biggest Christmas hit
Oklahoma	1949	Rogers and Hammerstein	First million-selling LP album
Rock Around the Clock	1955	Bill Haley and the Comets	Started rock 'n' roll craze
Please Please Me	1963	The Beatles	Their breakthrough single
Thriller	1983	Michael Jackson	Top-selling album
I Will Always Love You	1992	Whitney Houston	Top US single for 14 weeks
Three Lions on a Shirt	1996	Baddiel and Skinner	Most popular football song

▼ *The Spice Girls became the most successful girl-group ever with a succession of Top Ten hits from 1996 on. Their first album,* Spice, *was the biggest and fastest-selling debut album by a British group. More than 20 million people worldwide bought the album.*

POP SUPERSTARS' FIRST HITS		
Elvis Presley	*Heartbreak Hotel*	1956
Cliff Richard	*Move It*	1958
The Beatles	*Love Me Do*	1962
Elton John	*Your Song*	1970
Michael Jackson	*Got To Be There*	1971

▲ *The Backstreet Boys were named best newcomers of 1995. By 1999 they were listed as the biggest-earning American band, scooping £37 million in a year. Fame in the pop world can bring millionaire status.*

CANDLE IN THE WIND

● Elton John rewrote his song *Candle in the Wind* for the funeral of Princess Diana in 1997. It became the biggest-selling single ever, with worldwide sales of more than 33 million.

MOST NUMBER 1 SINGLES (UK)	
NAME	**No. 1s**
The Beatles	17
Elvis Presley	17
Cliff Richard	13
Madonna	10

(1= The Beatles, 1= Elvis Presley, 2 Cliff Richard, 3 Madonna)

▲ *Michael Jackson started his career at the age of five, singing in The Jackson Five with his older brothers. His* Thriller *album (1982) broke all records, and is reckoned to be the best-selling pop album of all time.*

▶ *Madonna, born Madonna Louise Ciccone, burst onto the pop scene in 1984 with her album* Like A Virgin. *She became the biggest-selling female singer in showbiz history. Her string of over 40 hits throughout the 1980s and 1990s made more than 100 million sales. The image she projects is often outrageous, and was as important as the sound of her music in rocketing her to superstardom.*

CURTAIN-UP!

The first theatre-goers were the ancient Greeks. They sat in audiences of up to 18,000 on hillsides to watch tragedies and comedies. The Romans built bigger stone theatres that could seat 40,000 and were used to stage raucous comedies. But the most successful playwright ever was William Shakespeare (1564–1616). His plays have been translated into numerous languages and are staged all over the world. Other performing arts besides drama are musicals, ballet and mime, in which actors use exaggerated movements instead of words to convey actions and emotions.

▲ *William Shakespeare wrote 37 plays. The longest is* Hamlet, *which also has the longest solo part. An actor playing Hamlet has 11,610 words to learn! More films have been made of Shakespeare's plays than any other playwright's.*

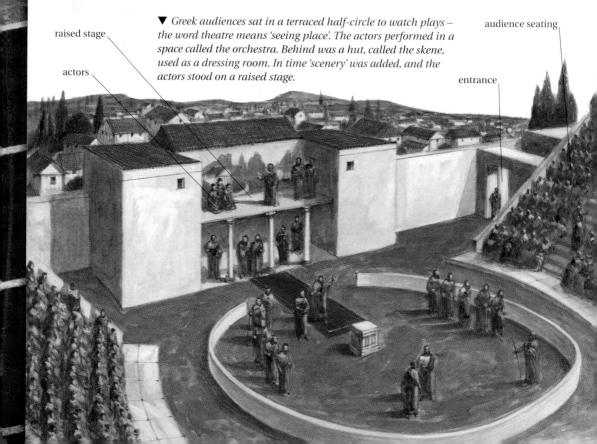

raised stage

actors

▼ *Greek audiences sat in a terraced half-circle to watch plays – the word theatre means 'seeing place'. The actors performed in a space called the orchestra. Behind was a hut, called the skene, used as a dressing room. In time 'scenery' was added, and the actors stood on a raised stage.*

audience seating

entrance

▼ *Broadway in New York is America's theatreland – the equivalent of London's West End – and is the place where British and American actors most want to perform. If a play transfers to Broadway from a West End theatre, and is praised by the critics, it is considered a hit.*

▲ *In ancient Greece, plays developed from religious ceremonies. Actors wore masks to show emotion – a happy face like this one for comedy, a gloomy one for tragedy.*

▶ *The Globe Theatre, built in 1599 beside the River Thames in London, is where William Shakespeare presented his plays. In 1613 the theatre burned down, but a replica Globe Theatre was opened in 1997 to stage Shakespeare's plays in the same way as they were originally performed.*

▶ *Ballet, originally a court entertainment in France, developed in the 1700s as a theatre show. Marie Taglioni (1804–84) made the ballerina the star of the ballet. Among the most famous ballet dancers were Rudolf Nureyev and Margot Fonteyn, who together once took 89 curtain calls for Swan Lake.*

▲ *In 1999 Andrew Lloyd Webber's* Cats *overtook* A Chorus Line *as the longest-running musical in New York. During the course of more than 6,000 performances it was seen by over 6 million people.*

»»	OLDEST DRAMATIC ARTS		
	ART FORM	DATE	COUNTRIES
1	Tragedy and comic drama	500 BC	Greece
2	Mime	100 BC	Rome, Italy
3	Opera	1580s	Italy and France
4	Ballet	1650s	France
5	Cinema	1890s	France and USA

FILM MAGIC

The film industry began in the early 1900s after experiments with 'kinetoscope' peepshows showed how much people loved watching moving pictures. The first big movie was D. W. Griffith's epic *Birth of a Nation*, made in 1915. The early films were silent – 'talkies' didn't appear until the late 1920s. Hollywood, California, became the home of American cinema, but today film-making is international.

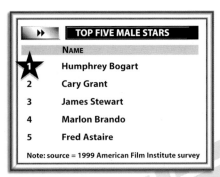

▶	TOP FIVE MALE STARS
	NAME
1	Humphrey Bogart
2	Cary Grant
3	James Stewart
4	Marlon Brando
5	Fred Astaire

Note: source = 1999 American Film Institute survey

▶	TOP FIVE FEMALE STARS
	NAME
1	Katherine Hepburn
2	Bette Davis
3	Audrey Hepburn
4	Ingrid Bergman
5	Greta Garbo

◀ *Voted the most popular film actor, Humphrey Bogart played tough-guy roles in 1940s films such as* Casablanca *and* The Maltese Falcon. *Bogart and Hepburn co-starred in* The African Queen, *for which Bogart won an Oscar in 1951.*

▲ *American actress Katherine Hepburn is the only star to have won four best-actress Oscars – an Oscar is the most sought-after award in the film industry. She won the first in 1933 and the last in 1981.*

◀ *Charlie Chaplin was the biggest star of the early silent screen. He shot to fame playing the baggy-trousered 'Little Tramp' in film comedies such as* The Kid *and* The Gold Rush. *Chaplin went on to become a successful composer, director, producer and screenwriter.*

▲ *Titanic (1997) is the only film since* Ben-Hur *(1959) to have won 11 oscars. More than 100 stunt artists helped to recreate the sinking scene, shown here in an artist's impression. The stunt team spent a record 6,000 hours on the set of* Titanic *– the equivalent of almost 17 years for one person!*

» Most costumes: 65 by Elizabeth Taylor in *Cleopatra*   » Biggest studio stage: Pinewood   » Most Oscars: Walt Disney

HOLLYWOOD

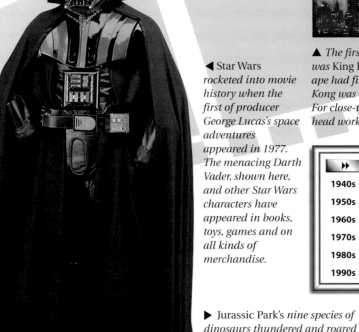

▲ Hollywood, California, was the home of American movies for most of the 20th century. Many of the greatest films ever were made in Hollywood studios.

◄ Star Wars rocketed into movie history when the first of producer George Lucas's space adventures appeared in 1977. The menacing Darth Vader, shown here, and other Star Wars characters have appeared in books, toys, games and on all kinds of merchandise.

▲ The first movie monster to become a star was King Kong (1933). Although the giant ape had film-goers on the edge of their seats, Kong was actually a model only 45 cm tall. For close-ups the studio used a giant furry head worked by three men inside!

►►	BLOCKBUSTERS BY DECADE	
1940s	**Gone With The Wind**	1939
1950s	**Ben-Hur**	1959
1960s	**The Sound Of Music**	1965
1970s	**Jaws**	1975
1980s	**ET: The Extra-Terrestrial**	1982
1990s	**Titanic**	1997

► Jurassic Park's *nine species of dinosaurs thundered and roared through the world's cinemas in 1993. Made of latex and foam rubber, the dinosaur robots were incredibly realistic. They included the largest film robot ever made – a 5.5-m tall Tyrannosaurus rex.*

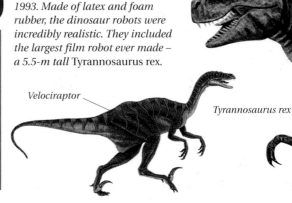

Velociraptor

Tyrannosaurus rex

►►	TOP FIVE FILMS	
	TITLE	YEAR
1	**Titanic**	1997
2	**Jurassic Park**	1993
3	**Independence Day**	1996
4	**Star Wars** series	1977–97
5	**The Lion King**	1994
Note: ranked by world box office takings		

CRAZES AND FADS

Crazes, or enthusiasms for doing something in a new way, come and go all the time. A fad is another word for a craze, though fads tend to last less time. Typical crazes are for weird hairstyles, startling dress, new foods, toys or games. Teddy bears started as a craze in the 1900s, and Action Men have been popular for about 40 years. More short-lived fads were Teenage Mutant Ninja Turtles and Power Rangers. Some crazes reappear years later, like yo-yos and scooters.

▲ *Yo-yos were a craze in the 1920s, the 1960s and again in the 1990s. 'Yo-yo' is said to be a Filipino word. In the Philippines people used yo-yos as weapons!*

CROSSWORDS

● The first crossword puzzle was published in the *New York World* newspaper of 1913. It had 32 clues. The crossword craze caught on, and general knowledge or cryptic crosswords now appear in most local and national newspapers.

● The largest crossword ever had more than 12,000 clues!

▲ *'Doing the Charleston' was the great dance craze of the 1920s. In the 1940s nations twirled to the Jitterbug, and later the Jive. Rock came in with a bang in the 1950s. The Twist was a dance of the 1960s and disco hit the 1970s. Salsa was a craze of 2000.*

▶ *Punk was a fad of 1970s youth culture and it started a craze for body art that is still popular. Ripped clothes, safety-pin piercings, chains, studs and spiky coloured hair were worn as an expression of freedom and a rebellion against conformity.*

◄ A kind of pinball machine was invented in the 1400s, long before electricity. The craze for pinball was particularly popular in Spain. Today 'amusement arcades' all over the world are filled with pinball games. Among the keenest gamblers are the Chinese.

▼ High-heeled shoes came into fashion in the 1600s and have never gone out. But in the 1970s they were given a new look with the platform heel. Platforms were often worn with flared trousers, which made a comeback in the 1990s.

◄ Tattooing is done mainly for fun, love, boldness or as body-art. Designs are pricked into the skin with needles dipped in coloured inks. The most tattooed person has covered 99.9 percent of his body in a leopard skin design.

► The first Barbie doll, whose full name is Barbara Millicent Roberts, went on sale in 1959, and the craze continues. There have been 2,000 different Barbie dolls to collect, dress and accessorize.

◄ Every few years a new craze comes along that everyone can do. The hula hoop is so simple that even toddlers can do it. All they have to do is wiggle! 'Hula' is the name of a dance from Hawaii that also requires wiggling (though not with hoops), and the name stuck!

ART AND SCULPTURE

Art ranges from tiny miniature paintings to whole buildings wrapped in plastic. The earliest-known art was made by Stone Age people, who painted pictures on cave walls and made figures from stone and clay. The ancient Egyptians and Chinese put some of their finest art treasures into tombs for the dead to take to the afterlife, and the ancient Greeks decorated their temples with statues of heroes and gods. The Italians gave painting a new, lifelike look from the late 1300s. Later, French Impressionists such as Claude Monet painted atmospheric scenes and abstract painters such as Picasso developed a non-realistic style called Cubism.

▲ *The Lascaux cave paintings in France are about 17,000 years old. Discovered in 1940, the cave walls are covered with paintings of animals like this wild horse.*

MOST EXPENSIVE WORKS OF ART		
By a man	Van Gogh's *Portrait Of Dr. Gachet*	£49.1 million
By a woman	Mary Cassatt's *In The Box*	£2.45 million
Sculpture	Canova's *The Three Graces*	£7.5 million
Photograph	Le Gray's *Grande Vague – Séte* (1855)	£507,500
Poster	Charles Rennie Mackintosh's poster advertising an art show, Glasgow	£68,200

▲ *John Constable (1776–1837) painted the landscape of eastern England, vividly capturing its clouds, trees, fields and the work of country people.*

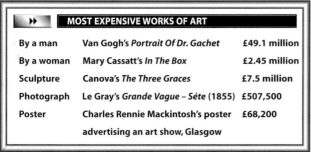

▼ *A few artists blast away at mountains to create mega-sculptures. This giant 172-m-high figure of the Sioux leader Crazy Horse is being carved on Thunderhead Mountain in South Dakota, USA.*

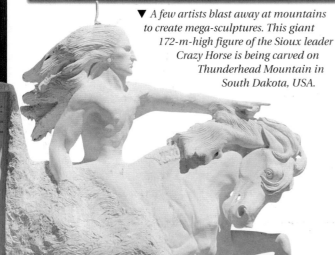

▲ *Italian artist Michelangelo (1475–1564) spent the years 1508–12 painting the ceiling of the Sistine Chapel in Rome. It includes the famous scene of God creating Adam, shown here in the centre of the picture.*

▼ *The Mona Lisa, by Leonardo da Vinci (1452–1519), is the world's most famous painting. In 1911 it was stolen from the Louvre Museum, Paris. Six fakes were sold to buyers before it was recovered in 1913.*

➤➤ GIANT STATUES AND FIGURES

Crazy Horse, stone figure*	Thunderhead Mountain, South Dakota, USA	172 m
Buddha, figure	Tokyo, Japan	120 m
The Motherland, statue	St Petersburg, Russia	82 m
The Long Man, chalk figure	Sussex, England	68 m
The Statue of Liberty	New York, USA	46 m

Note: * = begun in 1948, not yet complete

ART ON A GRAND SCALE

- The biggest painting is said to be one of Elvis Presley in Georgia, USA.
- The biggest art collection is in the Hermitage Museum, St Petersburg, Russia. It has more than 16,000 paintings.

▶ *The Dutch artist Rembrandt (1606–69), shown here in a self-portrait, left more than 2,000 paintings, etchings and drawings. He painted himself about 100 times, from youth to old age.*

▶ *The Venus de Milo, found on the island of Melos in Greece, was carved about 150 BC and is in the Louvre Museum, Paris. The famous statue shows the goddess of love, named Aphrodite by the Greeks and Venus by the Romans.*

➤➤ FAMOUS PAINTERS

Giotto (c.1266–1337)	Italian	Showed people in a more lifelike way
Leonardo da Vinci (1452–1519)	Italian	Painted the *Mona Lisa*
El Greco (1541–1614)	Spanish	Painted religious scenes
Rembrandt von Rijn (1606–69)	Dutch	Master of portraits
J. M. W. Turner (1775–1851)	English	Master of landscapes, seas and skies
Claude Monet (1840–1926)	French	Impressionist painter
Vincent Van Gogh (1853–90)	Dutch	Painted landscapes and portraits
Pablo Picasso (1881–1973)	Spanish	Many styles, including abstract Cubist

THEME PARKS AND FAIRS

The first fairs were markets where people met to buy and sell goods and enjoy street entertainments. Fairs were important in the Middle Ages. Later they developed into international World Fairs and Exhibitions. One of the most impressive was London's Great Exhibition of 1851, with more than 13,000 exhibits from around the world. The first big amusement park was Coney Island in the United States, which opened in the early 1900s. Theme parks such as Disneyland now attract tens of millions of thrill-seekers every year.

▲ *In 1851 a Great Exhibition was held in the magnificent, specially built Crystal Palace in London. It aimed to show people every known machine from around the world, and was a Victorian industrial theme park!*

◀ *Disney World in Florida is the biggest theme park in the world. The park's attractions recreate stories and cartoon characters, such as Dumbo the flying elephant, familiar from Disney films.*

▲ The London Eye, opened in 2000, is the world's largest observation wheel. From its slowly rotating gondolas, riders have a bird's eye view across London from 135 m above the ground.

▶ Acrobats are part of the fun of the circus. The most famous circus is Ringling Brothers and Barnum and Bailey's (combined in 1919). This circus had the biggest-ever Big Top, or tent, and its stars included the Wallendas, the only act to balance seven people in a human pyramid on a high wire.

▲ Roller-coaster rides like this one are not for the faint hearted! The fastest roller coaster ride is Superman The Escape, a thrill-a-second ride at Six Flags Magic Mountain in California, USA. Descending from 125 m, the cars reach 160 km/h!

GREATEST SHOWS ON EARTH

Most visitors	Disneyland, Tokyo, Japan with more than 17 million visitors a year
Most roller coasters	United States has 427; United Kingdom has 114
Biggest theme park	Disney World, Orlando, Florida, USA
Biggest g-force	The Mindbender at Galaxyland, Alberta, Canada reaches 6.3 g
First vertical-drop ride	Oblivion at Alton Towers, UK (1998); has a 55-m drop at over 100 km/h into a black hole!

TV AND DVD

The television (TV) age began in 1936, when only a few hundred people owned television sets and black-and-white pictures flickered across the screens. Today TV is the world's biggest form of information and entertainment. Satellite and cable networks provide hundreds of channels around the world, with thousands of hours of viewing. And if you miss your favourite film or programme the first time around, you can always watch it later on DVD.

▲ Satellite TV began in the 1960s with the first communications satellites in space. The first commercial TV satellite was Early Bird in 1965. Today a network of satellites circling Earth provides 24-hour live television around the world.

▼ TV talk-show host Oprah Winfrey is a bigger celebrity than many of the politicians and showbiz stars she interviews. She is also the richest TV entertainer in the world. Her talk-show was voted the best on TV for 11 seasons in a row and has won 30 Emmys, the most sought-after award for a US TV show.

▲ CNN is one of the world's biggest news broadcasters. Based in the USA, its news reporters can cover big stories such as a war, an election or a natural disaster anywhere in the world using mobile TV cameras and satellite links that keep them in contact with the studio. Using 23 satellites, CNN can reach 212 countries.

» Country with most videos: USA » Highest-paid TV actor: Jerry Seinfeld » Biggest cult TV show: *The X-Files*

►►	BIGGEST TV AUDIENCES IN THE UK		
	PROGRAMME	**YEAR**	**VIEWERS**
★1	Royal wedding, Prince Charles and Lady Diana Spencer	1981	39 million
2	World Cup, Brazil v England	1970	32.5 million
3	World Cup Final, England v West Germany	1966	32 million
4	Funeral of Diana, Princess of Wales	1997	31 million
5	*EastEnders* Christmas edition	1987	30 million

▼ *Prince Charles and Lady Diana Spencer's wedding was watched by millions in 1981. In 1997 Princess Diana's funeral was seen by about 2.5 billion people – more than a third of Earth's population.*

◄ *George Clooney is the most popular male TV star. During the 1996–97 season of the US hospital drama ER, Clooney was watched in Britain and the United States by more than 24 million people per episode, and was said to have been paid £92,000 for each one!*

▼ *Historic events such as the* Apollo Moon *landing of 1969 are seen by viewers 'live' as they take place. Millions of people watched as the astronauts took their first steps and posed for the camera.*

COUCH POTATOES!

● The country with the most TV sets is China with an estimated 394 million.
● The USA has about 227 million TV sets and the UK about 38 million.

▼ *Videotape, invented in the 1950s, has been superseded by DVD digital discs that give better quality sound and images. They are played on DVD players like this one. Films and children's TV shows are most popular.*

SPORT AND ENTERTAINMENT *QUIZ*

Now that you have read all about what's biggest and best in the world of Sport and Entertainment, see if you can answer these 20 quiz questions! (Pictures give clues, answers at the top of the page.)

◀ 3. Which country has won the most Olympic gold medals?

▶ 4. Which country has won the soccer World Cup the most times?

▼ 2. What is the name of Manchester United football team's home ground?

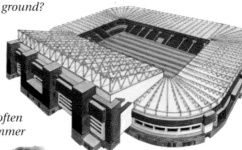

▲ 1. The game of polo was first played in which Asian country?

▼ 7. In which century was the jigsaw invented?

▼ 6. How often are the summer Olympic Games held?

▲ 5. Which country was the original home of the Olympic Games?

▲ 9. Who wrote Oliver Twist?

▶ 8. In which country did Ice hockey originate?

▶ 10. Name the reading system of raised dots used by blind people?

▼ 11. What is the name of the stone that helped scholars to understand hieroglyphics?

▼ 12. Who invented Europe's first printing press?

▼ 13. The guitar has its origins in which African country?

◄ 14. Which rock 'n' roll superstar was nicknamed 'the pelvis'?

◄ 15. Name the man who invented this instrument.

◄ 16. Who are the biggest-selling pop band ever?

▶ 17. Name this famous playwright.

▼ 19. Which famous painting was stolen in 1911?

▼ 20. Which famous statue, kept in the Louvre museum, has no arms?

▼ 18. Which film starred the biggest film robot?

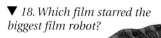

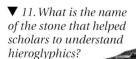

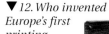

INDEX

Entries in bold refer to illustrations

*The publishers wish to thank the following artists
who have contributed to this book:*
Vanessa Card, Kuo Kang Chen, Terry Gabbey, Richard Hook, Rob Jakeway, John James, Janos Marffy,
Terry Riley, Eric Robson, Guy Smith, Roger Smith, Mike Taylor, Rudi Vizi, Mike White

The publishers wish to thank the following sourcesfor the photographs used in this book:
CORBIS: Page 8 (B/R) Reuters NewMedia Inc.; Page 9 (C) Kelly-Mooney Photography; Page 9 (B/L)
Ali Meyer; Page 10 (B/L) Jerry Cooke; Page 11 (B/L) Christian Liewig; Temp Sport; Page 12 (B/R)
Bettmann; Page 13 (B/L) Mike King; Page 14 (T) Raymond Gehman; Page 16 (T/L) Wally McNamee;
Page 17 (B/R) Reuters NewMedia Inc.; Page 21 (B) Richard Hamilton Smith; Page 22 (B/R)
Reuters NewMedia Inc.; Page 23 (T/L) S.I.N.; Page 23 (B/L) Bettmann; Page 23 (R) Henry Diltz;
Page 25 (C/L) Roger Wood; Page 25 (B/L) Reuters NewMedia Inc.; Page 27 (C/L) Roger Ressmeyer;
Page 27 (T/R) Bettmann; Page 28 (L) Hulton-Deutsch Collection; Page 28 (B/R)
Hulton-Deutsch Collection; Page 28 (T/R) Bettmann; Page 29 (T/L) Barry Lewis; Page 29 (C/L)
Earl & Nazima Kowall; Page 29 (C) Laura Dwight; Page 29 (R) Neal Preston; Page 30 (B/L) Bettmann;
Page 30 (B/R) Reuters NewMedia Inc.; Page 32 (T/R) Historical Picture Archive; Page 32 (B)
Morton Beebe, S.F.; Page 33 (T/L) Pawel Libera; Page 34 (C/L) Franz-Marc Frei; Page 34 (B)
Reuters NewMedia Inc.; Page 35 (C/L) Mitchell Gerber; Page 35 (C/R) Bettmann; Page 35 (B/R) AFP:
Creative Imprints: Page 16 (B); www.legomindstorms.com
All other photographs from Miles Kelly Archives.